BLOCKS
With
OPTIONS™

Edited by Carolyn S. Vagts

Annie's®

Introduction

Blocks With Options has everything you need to explore quick and easy quilt projects that can be adjusted to your needs. If you want a different size or want to see how a pattern will look in different colors, this is the book for you. Imagine **your** quilt **your** way.

Sometimes a quilter loves a certain pattern but can't imagine it in another color. Maybe the size of the quilt isn't what you want, but you're unsure about how to alter the quilt to the size you desire. These are easy fixes if you know how to make the changes, but if not, it can be frustrating. Every quilt you make should have a piece of your personality in it—whether it means changing the color or the size. Patterns are only guidelines and inspiration.

Blocks With Options is just that—inspirational! It contains 10 quilt projects, each with a different color option to inspire you to think outside the box. Several projects also have diagrams to show you how to increase or decrease the design to create differently sized projects. Once you experiment with color and size, you'll be amazed at how easy it is to change a pattern to accommodate your needs.

Enjoy!

Table of Contents

Flying Home Table Topper,
page 13

Blue Gardenia,
page 34

Wandering Paths Runner

Designed & Quilted by Julie Weaver

Two very simple block patterns strategically placed will create a stunning runner for a table or a bed.

Specifications

Skill Level: Confident Beginner
Runner Size: 54" x 18"
Block Size: 6" x 6" finished
Number of Blocks: 16

Materials

- ¼ yard blue plaid*
- ¼ yard medium blue print*
- ⅜ yard light blue print*
- ½ yard cream print*
- ¾ yard dark blue print*
- Thread
- Backing to size
- Batting to size*
- Basic sewing tools and supplies

Fabrics from Moda; cotton batting from The Warm Company.

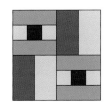

Wandering Paths
6" x 6" Finished Block
Make 16

Cutting

From blue plaid:
- Cut 4 (1½" by fabric width) F/G border strips.

From medium blue print:
- Cut 3 (2" by fabric width) E strips.

From light blue print:
- Cut 6 (1½" by fabric width) strips.
  Subcut into 64 (1½" x 3½") C rectangles.

From cream print:
- Cut 4 (1½" by fabric width) A strips.
- Cut 3 (2" by fabric width) D strips.

From dark blue print:
- Cut 2 (1½" by fabric width) B strips.
- Cut 4 (2½" by fabric width) H/I border strips.
- Cut 4 (2¼" by fabric width) strips for binding.

"I don't always use sashing in the quilts I make. I like it when you simply join the blocks and something totally unexpected happens. The premise of this book really did intrigue me—it's amazing that just turning a block or changing a fabric can make the same block, or set of blocks, so different. I think this is what makes quilting fun!" —Julie Weaver

Completing the Wandering Paths Blocks

1. Sew a B strip between two A strips along length to make an A-B-A strip set. Repeat to make two A-B-A strip sets.

2. Subcut the A-B-A strip sets into 32 (1½" x 3½") A-B-A segments as shown in Figure 1.

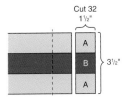

Cut 32
1½"

Figure 1

3. Sew a C rectangle to the top and bottom of each A-B-A segment as shown in Figure 2 to complete 32 quarter units.

Quarter Unit

Figure 2

4. Sew a D strip to an E strip along length to make D-E strip set. Repeat to make three D-E strip sets.

5. Subcut the D-E strip sets into 32 (3½") square D-E segments as shown in Figure 3.

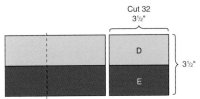

Cut 32
3½"

Figure 3

6. Join 2 D-E segments with two quarter units referring to the block diagram for placement to complete one block. Repeat to make a total of 16 blocks.

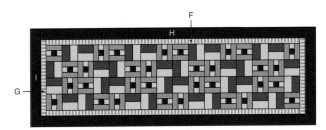

Wandering Paths Runner
Placement Diagram 54" x 18"

Completing the Runner

1. Arrange the blocks in two rows of eight blocks each referring to the Placement Diagram for the correct orientation of blocks. Join the rows to complete the pieced center; press.

2. Join the F/G strips on the short ends to make a long strip; press. Subcut strip into two 48½" F strips and two 14½" G strips.

3. Sew F strips to top and bottom, and G strips to the sides of the pieced center.

4. Join the H/I strips on the short ends to make a long strip; press. Subcut strip into two 50½" H strips and two 18½" I strips.

5. Sew H strips to the top and bottom, and I strips to the sides to complete the runner top.

6. Sandwich the batting between the pieced top and a prepared backing piece; baste layers together. Quilt as desired.

7. When quilting is complete, trim batting and backing fabric even with raw edges of the pieced top.

8. Prepare double-fold binding. Stitch binding to quilt front edges, mitering corners and overlapping ends. Fold binding to back side and stitch in place to finish. ■

Alternate Block Option

Shooting Stars

Designed & Quilted by Sandra L. Hatch

Three blocks and a fun border are all it takes to make this timeless table topper. Change the fabrics and you can have one for every season.

Specifications

Skill Level: Intermediate
Quilt Size: 48" x 48"
Block Size: 12" x 12" finished
Number of Blocks: 9

Materials

- ⅓ yard light blue print*
- ½ yard scroll flag print*
- ½ yard red/blue paisley*
- ¾ yard red print*
- ¾ yard navy print*
- ⅞ yard cream paisley*
- 1 yard cream solid*
- Backing to size
- Batting to size*
- Thread*
- Basic sewing tools and supplies

*Fabrics from Benartex; Blend batting from Fairfield; quilting thread from Coats.

Cross
12" x 12" Finished Block
Make 1

Corner
12" x 12" Finished Block
Make 4

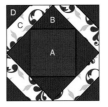

Framed Square
12" x 12" Finished Block
Make 4

Cutting

From light blue print:
- Cut 2 (3½" by fabric width) strips.
  Subcut into 22 (3½") E squares.

From scroll flag print:
- Cut 5 (2¼" by fabric width) binding strips.

From red/blue paisley:
- Cut 7 (2" by fabric width) strips.
  Subcut into 8 each 2" x 14" N strips and 2" x 20" P strips.

From red print:
- Cut 1 (6½" by fabric width) strip.
  Subcut into 4 (6½") A squares.
- Cut 4 (3½" by fabric width) strips.
  Subcut into 48 (3½") G squares.

From navy print:
- Cut 1 (5⅛" by fabric width) strip.
  Subcut into 8 (5⅛") squares; cut each square in half on 1 diagonal to make 16 B triangles.

- Cut 2 (3½" by fabric width) strips.
  Subcut into 16 (3½") D squares.
- Cut 5 (2" by fabric width) strips. Set aside 3 strips for I strips for H-I units.
  Subcut remaining strips into 24 (2") I squares and 4 (2" x 3½") L rectangles.

From cream paisley:
- Cut 2 (6⅞" by fabric width) strips.
  Subcut into 8 (6⅞") C squares; cut each square in half on 1 diagonal to make 16 C triangles.
- Cut 2 (6½" by fabric width) strips.
  Subcut into 20 (3½" x 6½") F rectangles and 2 (3⅞") squares. Cut each square in half on 1 diagonal to make 4 Q triangles.

From cream solid:
- Cut 12 (2" by fabric width) strips. Set aside 3 strips for H strips for H-I units.
  Subcut remaining strips into 8 strips each 2" x 12½" M and 2" x 18½" O, 16 (2" x 3⅞") J rectangles and 4 (2" x 3½") K rectangles.

8

Completing the Pieced Units

1. Sew an H strip to an I strip with right sides together along length to make an H-I strip set; press seams toward I. Repeat to make a total of three H-I strip sets.

2. Subcut the H-I strip sets into a total of 52 (2") H-I segments referring to Figure 1.

Cut 52
2"

Figure 1

3. Join two H-I segments to make an H-I unit as shown in Figure 2; press. Repeat to make a total of 26 H-I units.

Make 26

Figure 2

4. Draw a diagonal line from corner to corner on the wrong side of each G square.

5. Referring to Figure 3, place a G square right sides together on one corner of an F rectangle; stitch on the marked line. Trim seam allowance to ¼" and press G to the right side.

¼"

Figure 3

6. Add a second G square to the remaining end of F as in step 5 to complete one F-G unit as shown in Figure 4. Repeat to make a total of 20 F-G units.

¼"   Make 20

Figure 4

Completing the Cross Block

1. Select six H-I units, two E squares and four F-G units to make the Cross block.

2. Sew an E square to an H-I unit to make a row referring to Figure 5; press seams toward E. Repeat to make a second row.

Make 2

Figure 5

3. Join the rows to complete the block center as shown in Figure 6; press.

Figure 6

4. Sew an F-G unit to opposite sides of the block center to complete the center row as shown in Figure 7; press.

Figure 7

5. Sew an H-I unit to opposite ends of one F-G unit to make the top row as shown in Figure 8; press. Repeat to make the bottom row.

Figure 8

6. Sew the top and bottom rows to the block center to complete the Cross block as shown in Figure 9; press.

Figure 9

Completing the Corner Blocks

1. Select four each H-I units, F-G units and E squares to complete one Corner block.

2. Complete the block center and center row referring to steps 2–4 of Completing the Cross Block.

3. Join one each E square, F-G unit and H-I unit to make the top and bottom rows referring to Figure 10; press.

Figure 10

4. Sew the top and bottom rows to the block center to complete one Corner block referring to Figure 11; press.

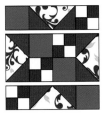

Figure 11

5. Repeat steps 1–4 to complete a total of four Corner blocks.

Completing the Framed Square Blocks

1. Mark a diagonal line from corner to corner on the wrong side of each D square.

2. Select one A square, four marked D squares and four each B and C triangles to complete one block.

3. Sew a B triangle to each side of A to make an A-B unit as shown in Figure 12; press seams toward B.

Figure 12

4. Sew a C triangle to each side of the A-B unit to complete an A-B-C unit as shown in Figure 13; press seams toward C.

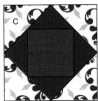

Figure 13

5. Referring to Figure 14, place a marked D square right sides together on each C corner and stitch on the marked line. Trim seams to ¼" and press D to the right side to complete one Framed Square block.

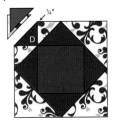

Figure 14

6. Repeat steps 2–5 to complete a total of four Framed Square blocks.

Completing the Quilt

1. Arrange and join the pieced blocks in three rows of three blocks each referring to the Assembly Diagram; press seams toward Framed Square blocks.

2. Join the rows to complete the pieced center.

3. Sew an I square to one end of an M strip and add J to make an M-I-J strip as shown in Figure 15; press seams toward I.

Figure 15

4. Repeat step 3 with an I square, J rectangle and an N strip to make an N-I -J strip, again referring to Figure 15.

5. Join the two strips to make an inner border strip as shown in Figure 16.

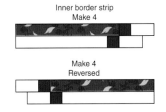

Figure 16

6. Repeat steps 3–5 to complete four inner border strips and four reversed inner border strips, again referring to Figure 16.

7. Trim the ends of each strip using the 45-degree line on a rotary ruler as shown in Figure 17.

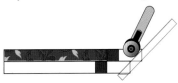

Figure 17

8. Join one each inner border strip and reversed inner border strip with a Q triangle to make an inner side border strip as shown in Figure 18; press. Repeat to make a total of four inner side border strips.

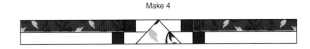

Figure 18

9. Sew an inner side border strip to opposite sides of the pieced center referring to the Assembly Diagram for positioning; press seams toward strip.

10. Sew an H-I unit to each end of each remaining inner side border strip; press. Sew these strips to the top and bottom of the pieced center, again referring to the Assembly Diagram, and press.

11. Sew an I square to one end of two O strips and join these strips on the I ends with a K rectangle to make an O-I-K strip referring Figure 19; press. Repeat to make a total of four strips.

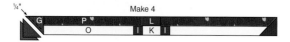

Figure 19

12. Join two P strips with an L rectangle to make an L-P strip, again referring to Figure 19; press. Repeat to make a total of four L-P strips.

13. Join one each O-I-K strip with one L-P strip to make a pieced strip; press.

14. Referring to Figure 19, place a G square right sides together at each end of the strip and stitch on the marked line; trim seam to ¼" and press G to the right side to complete one outer border strip. Repeat to make a total of four outer border strips.

15. Sew an outer border strip to opposite sides of the pieced center; press seams toward strips.

16. Sew an E square to each end of the remaining two outer border strips; press. Sew these strips to the top and bottom of the pieced center to complete the quilt top; press seams toward strips.

17. Sandwich the batting between the pieced top and a prepared backing piece; baste layers together. Quilt as desired.

18. When quilting is complete, trim batting and backing fabric even with raw edges of the pieced top.

19. Prepare double-fold binding. Stitch binding to quilt front edges, mitering corners and overlapping ends. Fold binding to back side and stitch in place to finish. ∎

"I have totes that hold decorative items for every major holiday or season. My tote for July Fourth is filled with red, white and blue patriotic things, including runners and wall quilts. I was looking for fabrics to make a specific size project for our celebration this year and found them in this pretty patriotic paisley print collection. The fabrics don't scream patriotic, and the subtle paisley prints make this fabric suitable for use at other times of the year." —Sandra Hatch

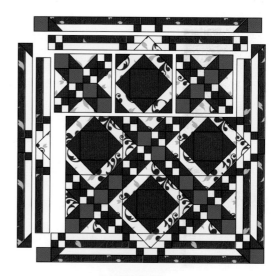

Shooting Stars
Assembly Diagram 48" x 48"

Alternate Block Options

Blocks With Options

Flying Home Table Topper

Designed & Quilted by Connie Rand

This table topper is all about the color placement.
Three block patterns and a simple double border will turn
your fabric into a charming table cover or wall hanging.

Specifications
Skill Level: Confident Beginner
Table Topper Size: 48" x 48"
Block Size: 12" x 12" finished
Number of Blocks: 9

Materials
- Scraps of 4 different green solids, tonals or prints from dark to light
- Scraps of 4 different gold solids, tonals or prints from dark to light
- ⅝ yard blue print
- 1⅛ yards gold print
- 1⅝ yards black solid
- Thread*
- Backing to size
- Batting to size
- Basic sewing tools and supplies

Quilting thread from Coats.

Triangles
12" x 12" Finished Block
Make 4

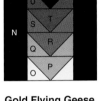

Gold Flying Geese
12" x 12" Finished Block
Make 2

Green Flying Geese
12" x 12" Finished Block
Make 2

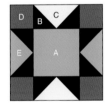

Star
12" x 12" Finished Block
Make 1

Cutting
Note: Sort and label same color family scraps into 4 groups from dark to light before cutting.

From green scraps:
Fabric 1 (dark):
- Cut 4 (3½") L squares.
- Cut 2 (3½" x 6½") K rectangles.

Fabric 2 (medium dark):
- Cut 4 (3½") J squares.
- Cut 2 (3½" x 6½") I rectangles.

Fabric 3 (medium light):
- Cut 4 (3½") H squares.
- Cut 2 (3½" x 6½") G rectangles.

Fabric 4 (light):
- Cut 1 (6½") A square.
- Cut 4 (3½") F squares.
- Cut 2 (3½" x 6½") E rectangles.

From gold scraps:
Fabric 1 (dark):
- Cut 4 (3½") U squares.
- Cut 2 (3½" x 6½") T rectangles.

Fabric 2 (medium dark):
- Cut 4 (3½") S squares.
- Cut 2 (3½" x 6½") R rectangles.

Fabric 3 (medium light):
- Cut 4 (3½") Q squares.
- Cut 2 (3½" x 6½") P rectangles.

Fabric 4 (light):
- Cut 4 (3½") O squares.
- Cut 2 (3½" x 6½") C rectangles.

From blue print:
- Cut 1 (3½" by fabric width) strip. Subcut into 8 (3½") D squares.
- Cut 1 (12⅞" by fabric width) strip. Subcut 2 (12⅞") squares. Cut each square on 1 diagonal to make 4 V triangles.

14

From gold print:
- Cut 5 (3½" by fabric width) strips.
  Subcut into 4 (3½") Z squares and
  4 (3½" x 36½") X strips.
- Cut 5 (2¼" by fabric width) strips for binding.

From black solid:
- Cut 9 (3½" by fabric width) strips.
  Subcut into 8 (3½") B squares, 4 (3½" x 6½")
  M rectangles, 8 (3½" x 12½") N strips and
  4 (3½" x 42½") Y strips.
- Cut 1 (12⅞" by fabric width) strip.
  Subcut 2 (12⅞") squares. Cut each square on
  1 diagonal to make 4 W triangles.

Completing the Blocks
1. Draw a diagonal line from corner to corner on the wrong side of each B, F, H, J, L, O, Q, S and U square.

2. Place a B square, right sides together, on one end of a C rectangle. Stitch on the marked line and trim ¼" from the stitching as shown in Figure 1. Repeat with a second B square on the opposite end to make a B-C Flying Geese unit, again referring to Figure 1.

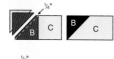

Figure 1

3. Repeat step 2 to make two each Flying Geese units as shown in Figure 2.

Make 2 each

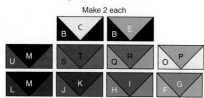

Figure 2

4. Join four gold Flying Geese units, in order from dark to light, as shown in Figure 3. Repeat to make two gold Flying Geese strips.

Make 2 each

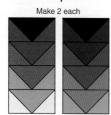

Figure 3

5. Join four green Flying Geese units in same manner as in step 4, again referring to Figure 3. Repeat to make two green Flying Geese strips.

6. Sew N strips to each side of the pieced Flying Geese strips referring to block diagrams to complete two each Gold and Green Flying Geese blocks.

7. Referring to Figure 4 to make the Star block, sew D squares on the ends of the two B-C Flying Geese units to make the top and bottom rows. Sew the B-E Flying Geese units to opposite sides of the A square. Sew the top and bottom rows to the center row to complete one Star block.

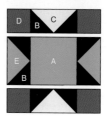

Figure 4

8. Join the V and W triangles along the diagonal sides to make four Triangles blocks referring to the block diagram.

Completing the Table Topper
1. Arrange and join the blocks referring to the Assembly Diagram for placement and orientation.

2. Sew an X strip to each side of the quilt center. Sew a D square to each end of two X strips and sew to the top and bottom of the quilt center.

3. Sew a Y strip to each side of the pieced quilt. Sew a Z square to each end of two Y strips and sew to the top and bottom to finish the topper.

4. Sandwich the batting between the pieced top and a prepared backing piece; baste layers together. Quilt as desired.

5. When quilting is complete, trim batting and backing fabric even with raw edges of the pieced top.

6. Prepare double-fold binding. Stitch binding to quilt front edges, mitering corners and overlapping ends. Fold binding to back side and stitch in place to finish. ∎

"I wanted to use dark to light shades of the green and yellow fabrics to represent motion toward the center of the quilt." —Connie Rand

Flying Home Table Topper
Assembly Diagram
48" x 48"

Alternate Block Options

Tipsie Geese

Design by Carol Streif
Quilted by Leanna Spanner

Two traditional blocks can be turned in several ways to create many different looks. This is only one way to set these blocks.

Specifications
Skill Level: Intermediate
Quilt Size: 55½" x 74½"
Block Size: 9½" x 9½" finished
Number of Blocks: 33

Materials
- ⅜ yard dark red print*
- ¾ yard green print*
- 2⅝ yards cream tonal*
- 2¾ yards red print*
- Thread
- Backing to size
- Batting to size*
- Template material
- Basic sewing tools and supplies

Fabrics from Northcott; Fairfield batting.

Cutting

From dark red print:
- Cut 6 (1⅝" by fabric width) strips.
    Subcut into 44 E pieces, 44 F pieces and 22 C pieces using patterns provided.

From green print:
- Cut 6 (1⅝" by fabric width) strips.
    Subcut into 44 E pieces, 44 F pieces and 22 C pieces using patterns provided.
- Cut 6 (1½" by fabric width) strips for J/K borders.

From cream tonal:
- Cut 4 (2" by fabric width) strips.
    Subcut into 44 D pieces using pattern provided.
- Cut 3 (2¼" by fabric width) strips.
    Subcut into 88 H pieces using pattern provided.
- Cut 3 (1¾" by fabric width) strips.
    Subcut into 176 G pieces using pattern provided.
- Cut 6 (10" by fabric width) strips.
    Subcut 24 (10") squares. Cut 22 A pieces using pattern provided. Set aside the remaining 10" squares for setting blocks.

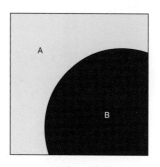

Drunkard's Path
9½" x 9½" Finished Block
Make 22

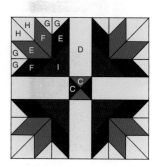

Goose Tracks
9½" x 9½" Finished Block
Make 11

From red print:
- Cut 2 (3" by fabric width) strips.
    Subcut into 44 I pieces using template.
- Cut 1 (8" by fabric width) strip.
    Subcut into 4 (8") squares. Subcut each square into a B piece using pattern provided.
- Use the remaining fabric length to cut the following strips:
    Cut 4 (3½" x 74") strips for L/M borders.
    Cut 4 (2¼" x 74") strips for binding.
    Cut 2 (8" x 74") strips. Subcut into 18 (8") squares. Subcut each square into a B piece using pattern provided.

Completing the Drunkard's Path Blocks
1. Make 22 Drunkard's Path blocks using the A and B pieces referring to the Curved Piecing tutorial on page 20.

Completing the Goose Tracks Blocks
1. Sew G to a dark red E as shown in Figure 1; press seam toward E.

Figure 1

Figure 2

2. Sew G to a green F as shown in Figure 2; press seam toward G.

3. Join the E-G unit to the F-G unit as shown in Figure 3; press seam open. Add H to short edge of F; press seam toward H.

Figure 3

4. Repeat steps 1–3 using a green E and a dark red F referring to Figure 4.

Figure 4

5. Join the two E-F-G-H units matching green sides together as shown in Figure 5. Add I to complete one corner unit.

Figure 5

6. Repeat steps 1–5 to make 4 corner units.

7. Join a dark red C and green C along short sides as shown in Figure 6; press seam toward green. Repeat to make a second unit. Join units together to form a center unit, again referring to Figure 6.

Figure 6

8. Sew D to opposite sides of the center unit as shown in Figure 7 to complete the middle row of the block.

Figure 7

9. Sew D between two corner units as shown in Figure 8 to make a top row. Press seam toward D. Repeat to make a bottom row.

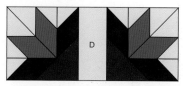

Figure 8

10. Complete the block by sewing the rows together referring to the block diagram.

11. Repeat steps 1–10 to complete a total of 11 Goose Tracks blocks.

Completing the Quilt

1. Arrange the blocks and the two 10" cream tonal setting squares in seven rows of five blocks each referring to the Assembly Diagram for positioning; pay close attention to the orientation of the Drunkard's Path blocks.

2. Join the blocks in each row, and then join rows together to complete the pieced center.

3. Join the J/K strips on short ends to make one strip. Subcut the strip into two 67" J strips and two 50" K strips. Sew the J strips to the sides and the K strips to the top and bottom of pieced center.

4. Trim the L/M border strips to make two 69" L strips and two 56" M strips. Sew the L strips to the sides and the M strips to the top and bottom of the pieced center.

5. Sandwich the batting between the pieced top and a prepared backing piece; baste layers together. Quilt as desired.

6. When quilting is complete, trim batting and backing fabric even with raw edges of the pieced top.

7. Prepare double-fold binding. Stitch binding to quilt front edges, mitering corners and overlapping ends. Fold binding to back side and stitch in place to finish. ∎

"I love traditional patterns, but I also love contemporary quilts. This seemed to be a good in-between solution."
—Carol Streif

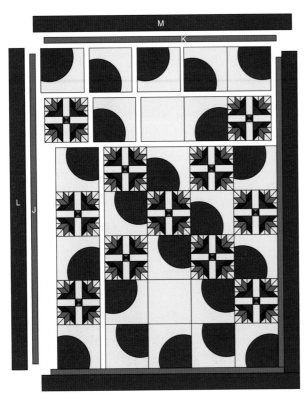

Tipsie Geese
Assembly Diagram 55½" x 74½"

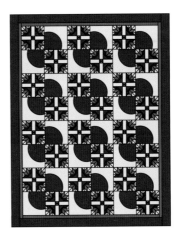

Tipsie Geese
Alternate Placement Diagram 65" x 80½"
*To create this new layout, make 24 of each
block. Arrange in 8 rows of 6 blocks
as shown adding the same borders on the
original layout. Be sure to purchase
additional fabric.*

Alternate Block Options

Curved Piecing

There are many traditional quilt blocks and free-form designs that use curves. Like many other quilting techniques, a few tips and a little practice will make curved piecing less of a struggle and open up your design choices.

Careful cutting and marking of curved pieces is critical to having a smooth curved seam. Curved seams are bias edges and will stretch easily without careful handling.

Curves With Templates

Make templates from template plastic or freezer paper for traditional blocks. You can also purchase acrylic templates for most common curved shapes in different sizes. Or, use a die-cut system to cut multiple shapes accurately.

Be sure to follow the template as closely as possible when cutting pieces. If using a rotary blade, use the smallest rotary blade size available to easily negotiate the curves. If using scissors, move the fabric/template instead of the scissors when cutting. Be sure your scissors are sharp.

Find the centers of both the convex (outer curve) and concave (inner curve) edges by folding the pieces in half, finger-press and mark with a pin. Purchased templates and die-cut pieces should have center notches. Match the centers and pin with the convex curve on the top referring to the Drunkard's Path block in Figure A.

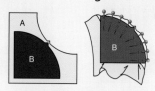

Figure A

Match and pin the seam ends. Then pin liberally between the seam ends and center, matching the seam edges and referring again to Figure A.

Slowly stitch pieces together an inch or two at a time, removing pins and keeping seam edges even.

Clip only the concave seam allowance if necessary. Press seam allowances flat toward the concave curve (Figure B).

Figure B

Common traditional blocks like Apple Core and Rob Peter to Pay Paul are constructed in the same manner.

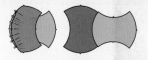

Apple Core

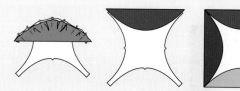

Rob Peter to Pay Paul

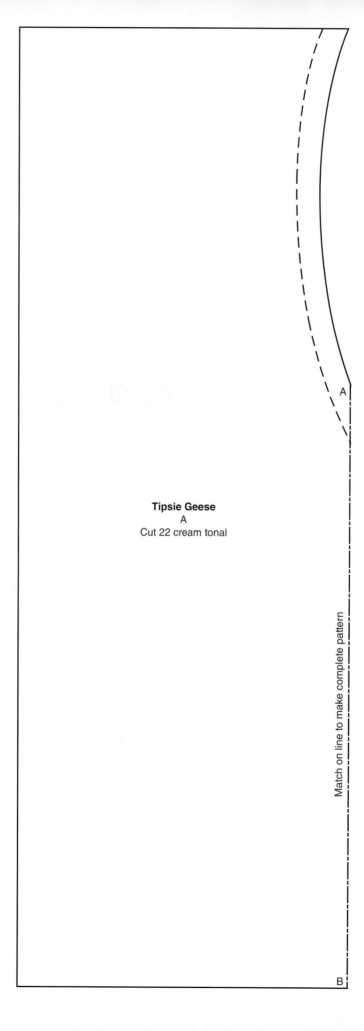

Tipsie Geese
A
Cut 22 cream tonal

Match on line to make complete pattern

A

B

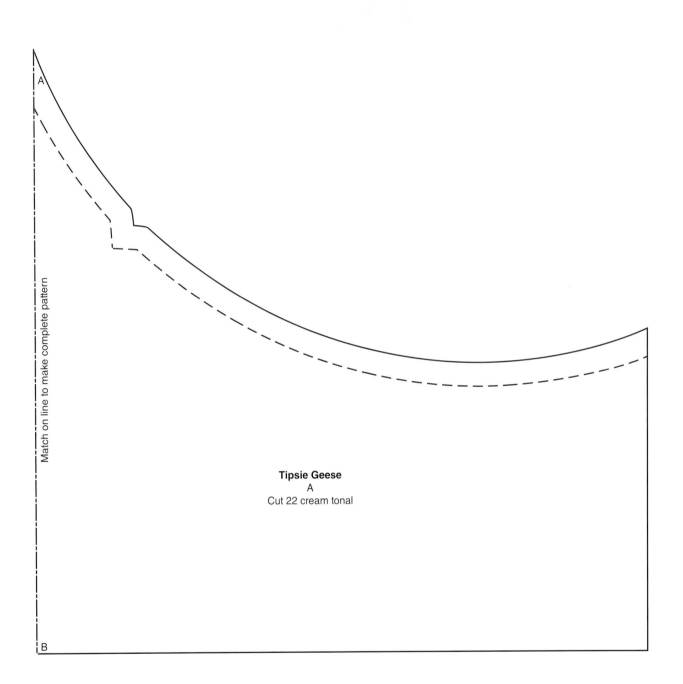

Match on line to make complete pattern

A

B

Tipsie Geese
A
Cut 22 cream tonal

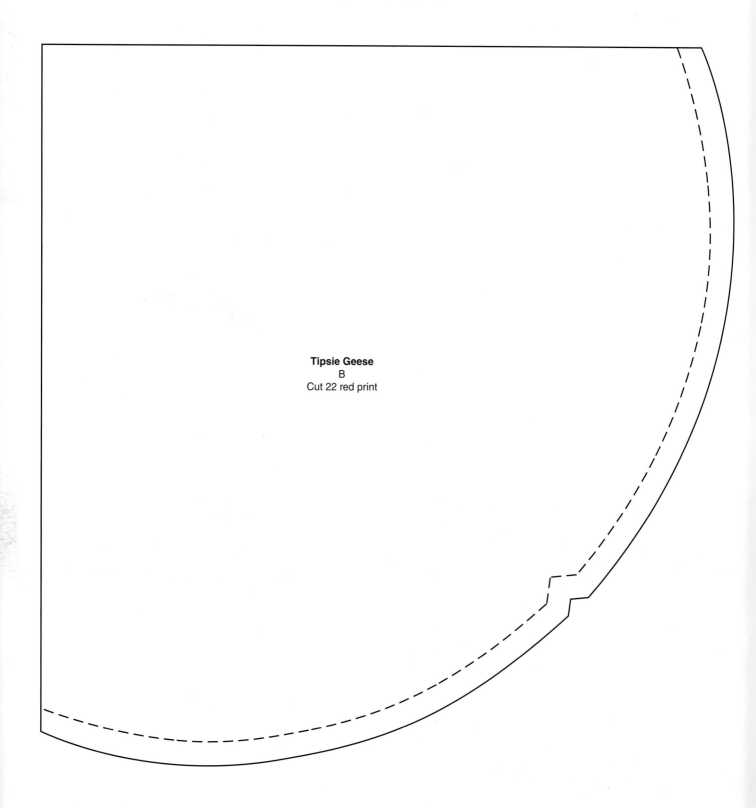

Tipsie Geese
B
Cut 22 red print

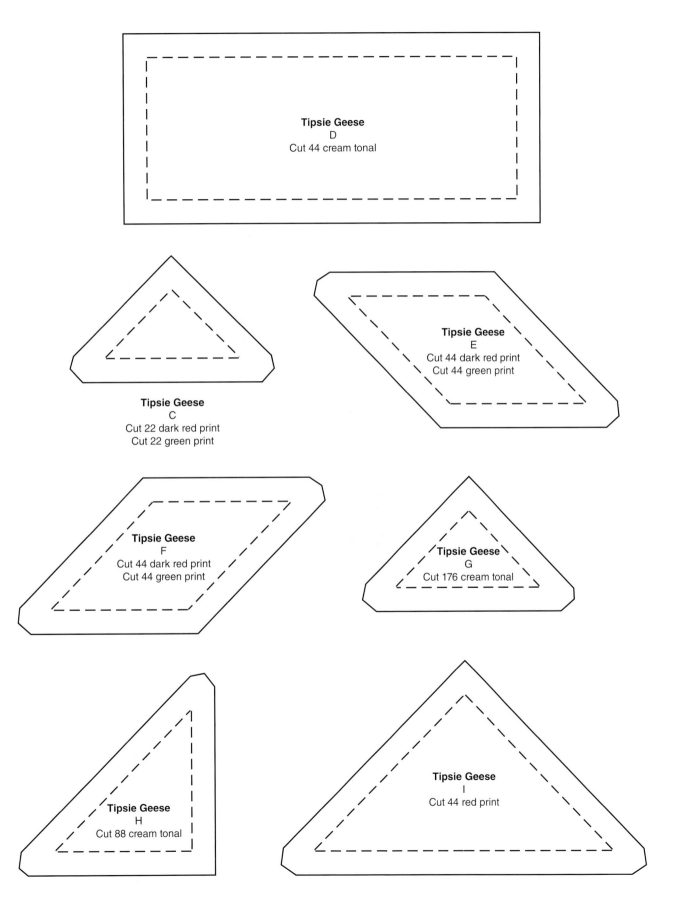

Tipsie Geese
D
Cut 44 cream tonal

Tipsie Geese
C
Cut 22 dark red print
Cut 22 green print

Tipsie Geese
E
Cut 44 dark red print
Cut 44 green print

Tipsie Geese
F
Cut 44 dark red print
Cut 44 green print

Tipsie Geese
G
Cut 176 cream tonal

Tipsie Geese
H
Cut 88 cream tonal

Tipsie Geese
I
Cut 44 red print

Fish Tails

Design by Gina Gempesaw
Quilted by Carole Whaling

This quick and easy quilt pattern can be made in a variety of fun colors. With planned placement, you will have a school of delightful fish.

Specifications
Skill Level: Intermediate
Quilt Size: 66" x 90"

Materials
- ¾ yard yellow tonal
- 1½ yards total assorted green prints or at least 6 fat quarters
- 1½ yards total assorted blue prints or at least 6 fat quarters
- 1⅔ yards dark blue tonal
- 2⅞ yards light blue tonal
- Thread
- Backing to size
- Batting to size
- Basic sewing tools and supplies

Cutting

From yellow tonal:
- Cut 4 (5⅛" by fabric width) strips.
  Subcut into 29 (5⅛") squares; cut each square in half on 1 diagonal to make 58 E triangles.

From assorted green prints:
- Cut 6 (13¼") squares.
  Subcut each square on both diagonals to make 24 A triangles. Discard 3 triangles.
- Cut 14 (9⅜" x 4¾") rectangles.
  With right sides up, cut a triangle off at a 45-degree angle on one end of each rectangle as shown in Figure 1 to make 14 B trapezoids.

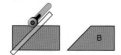

Figure 1

From assorted blue prints:
- Cut 6 (13¼") squares.
  Subcut each square on both diagonals to make 24 C triangles. Discard 3 triangles.

- Cut 14 (9⅜" x 4¾") rectangles.
  With right sides up, cut a triangle off at a 45-degree angle on one end of each rectangle referring to Figure 1 to make 14 D trapezoids.

From dark blue tonal:
- Cut 8 (3½" by fabric width) H/I strips.
- Cut 8 (2¼" by fabric width) strips for binding.

From light blue tonal:
- Cut 4 (13¼" by fabric width) strips.
  Subcut into 10 (13¼") squares. Cut each square along both diagonals to make 40 F triangles.
- Cut 8 (4¾" by fabric width) strips.
  Subcut into 30 (9⅜" x 4¾") rectangles. With right sides up, cut a triangle off at a 45-degree angle on one end of each rectangle referring to Figure 1 to make 30 G trapezoids.

Completing the Quilt Center
1. Join an E triangle with a B trapezoid to make a B-E triangle (Figure 2). Repeat to make a total of 14 B-E triangles.

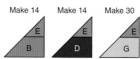

Figure 2

2. Join an E triangle with a D trapezoid to make an E-D triangle, again referring to Figure 2. Repeat to make a total of 14 D-E triangles.

3. Join an E triangle with a G trapezoid to make a G-E triangle, again referring to Figure 2. Repeat to make a total of 30 G-E triangles.

4. Select seven F triangles, three G-E triangles, two each D-E and B-E triangles, and three each A and C triangles to make Row 1.

5. Arrange the selected triangles to make one Row 1 referring to Figure 3, grouping the triangles in sets of four to create five square blocks. Match fabrics in the B-E and D-E triangles with the adjacent A and C triangles respectively.

Make 1
Row 1

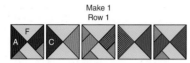

Figure 3

6. Sew each four-triangle arrangement together to create five blocks. Join the blocks to complete Row 1.

7. Select six F triangles, four G-E triangles, two each D-E and B-E triangles, and three each A and C triangles to make Row 2.

8. Arrange the selected triangles to make one Row 2 referring to Figure 4, grouping the triangles in sets of four to create five square blocks. Match fabrics in the B-E and D-E triangles with the adjacent A and C triangles respectively.

Make 3
Row 2

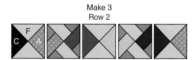

Figure 4

9. Sew each four-triangle arrangement together to create five blocks. Join the blocks to complete one Row 2.

10. Repeat steps 7–9 to make three of Row 2.

11. Select four F triangles, six G-E triangles, two each D-E and B-E triangles and three each A and C triangles to make Row 3.

12. Arrange the selected triangles to make one Row 3 referring to Figure 5, grouping the triangles in sets of four to create five square blocks. Match fabrics in the B-E and D-E triangles with the adjacent A and C triangles respectively.

Make 2
Row 3

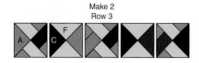

Figure 5

13. Sew each four-triangle arrangement together to create five blocks. Join the blocks to complete Row 3.

14. Repeat steps 11–13 to make a second Row 3.

15. Select seven F triangles, three G-E triangles, two each D-E and B-E triangles, and three each A and C triangles to make Row 4.

16. Arrange the selected triangles to make one Row 4 referring to Figure 6, grouping the triangles in sets of four to create five square blocks. Match fabrics in the B-E and D-E triangles with the adjacent A and C triangles respectively.

Make 1
Row 4

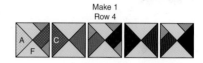

Figure 6

17. Sew each four-triangle arrangement together to create five blocks. Join the blocks to complete Row 4.

18. Arrange the rows as shown in Figure 7. Join rows to complete the quilt center.

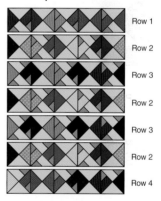

Row 1
Row 2
Row 3
Row 2
Row 3
Row 2
Row 4

Figure 7

Completing the Quilt

1. Join the H/I strips on the short ends to make a long strip; press. Subcut strip into two 84½" H strips and two 66½" I strips.

2. Sew H strips to opposite sides and I strips to the top and bottom of the pieced center.

3. Sandwich the batting between the pieced top and a prepared backing piece; baste layers together. Quilt as desired.

4. When quilting is complete, trim batting and backing fabric even with raw edges of the pieced top.

5. Prepare double-fold binding. Stitch binding to quilt front edges, mitering corners and overlapping ends. Fold binding to back side and stitch in place to finish. ■

"A school of tropical fish inspired this quilt." —Gina Gempesaw

Alternate Block Option

Fish Tails
Placement Diagram 66" x 90"

Cobblestone Path

Designed & Quilted by Julie Weaver

Using two different 6-inch blocks can provide many options for inspiring quilts. Here's one you can easily make larger or smaller by simply adding or removing a row.

Specifications
Skill Level: Confident Beginner
Quilt Size: 48" x 60"
Block Size: 6" x 6" finished
Number of Blocks: 63

Materials
- ⅜ yard medium tan print 1*
- ⅝ yard light tan print*
- ⅝ yard medium tan print 2*
- 1 yard red print 2*
- 1⅜ yards cream print*
- 1½ yards red print 1*
- Thread
- Backing to size
- Batting to size*
- Basic sewing tools and supplies

Fabrics from Moda; Thermore batting from Hobbs.

Cutting

From medium tan print 1:
- Cut 5 (2" by fabric width) K/L strips

From light tan print:
- Cut 6 (3" by fabric width) I strips.

From medium tan print 2:
- Cut 6 (3" by fabric width) J strips.

From red print 2:
- Cut 6 (2" by fabric width) M/N strips.
- Cut 6 (2¼" by fabric width) strips for binding.

From cream print:
- Cut 8 (1½" by fabric width) A strips.
- Cut 5 (2½" by fabric width) C strips.
- Cut 3 (3½" by fabric width) E strips.
- Cut 2 (3" by fabric width) G strips.

From red print 1:
- Cut 8 (1½" by fabric width) B strips.
- Cut 5 (2½" by fabric width) D strips.
- Cut 3 (3½" by fabric width) F strips.
- Cut 2 (4" by fabric width) H strips.

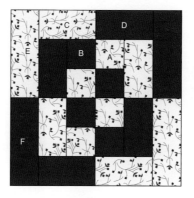

Cobblestone Path A
6" x 6" Finished Block
Make 32

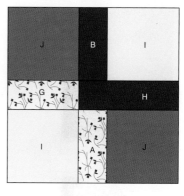

Cobblestone Path B
6" x 6" Finished Block
Make 31

Completing the Cobblestone Path A Blocks

1. Sew an A strip to a B strip along length to make an A-B strip set. Repeat to make a total of five A-B strip sets.

2. Subcut the A-B strip sets into 128 (1½" x 2½") A-B segments as shown in Figure 1.

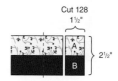

Figure 1

3. Join two A-B segments, with opposite colors touching, to make a Four-Patch unit as shown in Figure 2. Repeat to make a total of 64 Four-Patch units.

Figure 2

Figure 3

4. Join two Four-Patch units, with opposite colors touching, to make an Eight-Patch unit as shown in Figure 3. Repeat to make a total of 32 Eight-Patch units.

5. Sew a C strip to a D strip along length to make C-D strip set. Repeat to make a total of five C-D strip sets.

6. Subcut the C-D strip sets into 128 (1½" x 4½") C-D segments as shown in Figure 4.

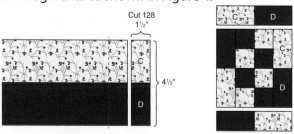

Figure 4   **Figure 5**

7. Sew C-D segments to opposite sides of each Eight-Patch unit and then to the top and bottom of unit as shown in Figure 5.

8. Sew an E strip to an F strip along length to make an E-F strip set. Repeat to make a total of three E-F strip sets.

9. Subcut the E-F strip sets into 64 (1½" x 6½") E-F segments as shown in Figure 6.

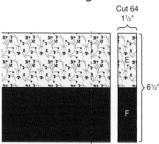

Figure 6

10. Sew E-F segments to two opposite sides of each pieced unit, referring to the block drawing for positioning, to complete all Cobblestone Path A blocks.

Completing the Cobblestone Path B Blocks

1. Sew a G strip to an H strip along length to make a G-H strip set. Repeat to make two G-H strip sets.

2. Subcut the G-H strip sets into 31 (1½" x 6½") G-H segments as shown in Figure 7.

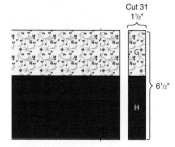

Figure 7

3. Sew an A strip between an I and J strip along length to make an I-A-J strip set. Repeat to make three I-A-J strip sets.

4. Subcut the I-A-J strip sets into 31 (3" x 6½") I-A-J segments as shown in Figure 8.

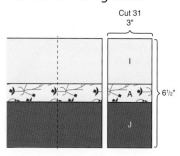

Figure 8

5. Join an I-A-J segment to a G-H segment referring to Figure 9 for placement. Repeat to make 31 units.

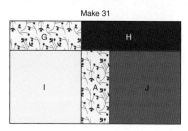

Figure 9

6. Sew a B strip between an I and J strip along length to make an I-B-J strip set. Repeat to make three I-B-J strip sets.

7. Subcut the I-B-J strip sets into 31 (3" x 6½") I-B-J segments as shown in Figure 10.

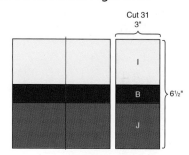

Figure 10

8. Sew an I-B-J segment to opposite sides of the G-H segment of the pieced unit referring to the block drawing for placement. Repeat to complete 31 Cobblestone Path B blocks.

Completing the Quilt

1. Arrange and join the Cobblestone Path A and Cobblestone Path B blocks in nine rows of seven blocks each, referring to the Assembly Diagram for the correct orientation of the blocks. Join the rows to complete the pieced center; press.

2. Join the K/L strips on the short ends to make a long strip; press. Subcut strip into two 54½" K strips and two 45½" L strips.

3. Sew K strips to opposite sides and L strips to the top and bottom of the pieced center.

4. Join the M/N strips on the short ends to make a long strip; press. Subcut strip into two 57½" M strips and two 48½" N strips.

5. Sew M strips to opposite sides and N strips to the top and bottom to complete the quilt top.

6. Sandwich the batting between the pieced top and a prepared backing piece; baste layers together. Quilt as desired.

7. When quilting is complete, trim batting and backing fabric even with raw edges of the pieced top.

8. Prepare double-fold binding. Stitch binding to quilt front edges, mitering corners and overlapping ends. Fold binding to back side and stitch in place to finish. ■

"I like it when you simply join the blocks and something totally unexpected happens. It's amazing that just turning a block or changing a fabric can make the same block, or set of blocks, look so different. I think this is what makes quilting fun!" —Julie Weaver

Alternate Block Option

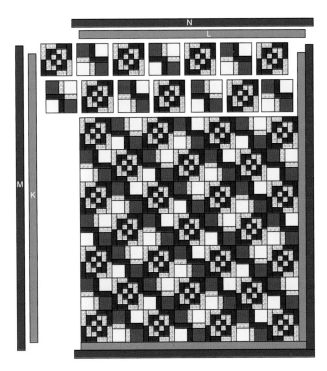

Cobblestone Path
Assembly Diagram 48" x 60"

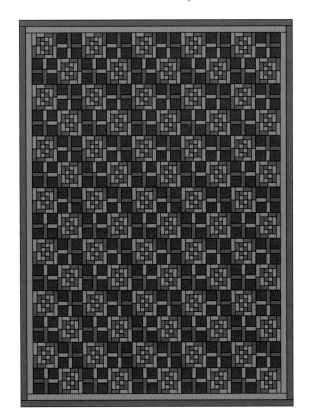

Cobblestone Path
Alternate Placement Diagram 66" x 90"
To create this twin-size quilt, make 70 blocks each of Cobblestone Path A and B blocks. Try new colors and a new orientation of the Cobblestone Path B blocks for a different look. Be sure to purchase additional fabric.

Blue Gardenia

Design by Lyn Brown
Quilted by Jami Goto

Two blocks that are nearly the same were used to create a dynamic quilt that's perfect for any color combination.

Specifications

Skill Level: Intermediate
Quilt Size: 80" x 80"
Block Size: 12" x 12" finished
Number of Blocks: 25

Materials

- 1¾ yards bright green batik*
- 2 yards dark teal batik*
- 2¾ yards aqua batik*
- 3 yards white batik*
- Thread
- Backing to size
- Batting to size
- Basic sewing tools and supplies

**All fabrics from Hoffman California Fabrics.*

Cutting

From bright green batik:

- Cut 2 (2⅞" by fabric width) strips.
  Subcut into 26 (2⅞") squares. Cut each square on 1 diagonal to make 52 F triangles.
- Cut 3 (7½" by fabric width) strips.
  Subcut into 13 (7½") B squares.
- Cut 1 (2½" by fabric width) strip.
  Subcut into 4 (2½") L squares.
- Cut 7 (2½" by fabric width) strips for O borders.

From dark teal batik:

- Cut 5 (3⅜" by fabric width) strips.
  Subcut into 52 (3⅜") C squares.
- Cut 4 (2½" by fabric width) strips.
  Subcut into 48 (2½") J squares.
- Cut 2 (2⅞" by fabric width) strips.
  Subcut into 24 (2⅞") squares. Cut each square on 1 diagonal to make 48 K triangles.
- Cut 9 (2½" by fabric width) strips for binding.

From aqua batik:

- Cut 3 (3⅜" by fabric width) strips.
  Subcut into 25 (3⅜") D squares.
- Cut 3 (7½" by fabric width) strips.
  Subcut into 13 (7½") A squares.

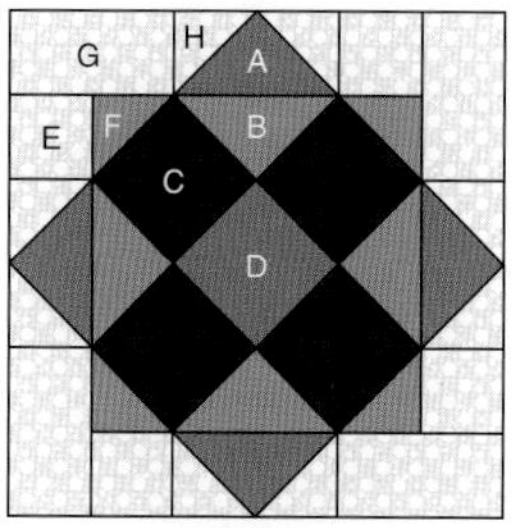

Dark Gardenia
12" x 12" Finished Block
Make 13

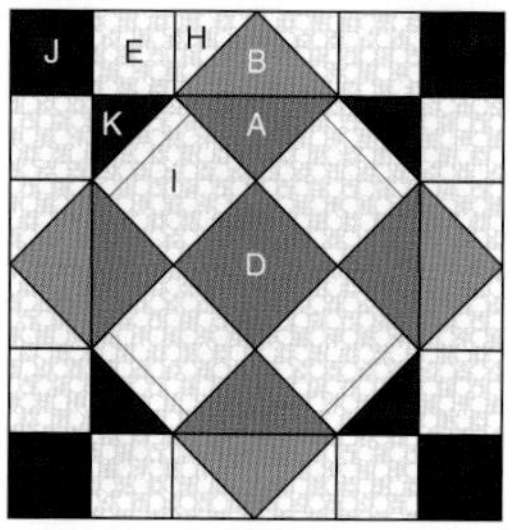

Light Gardenia
12" x 12" Finished Block
Make 12

- Cut 1 (2½" by fabric width) strip.
  Subcut into 4 (2½") M squares.
- Cut 8 (6½" by fabric width) strips for P/Q borders.

From white batik:

- Cut 4 (4½" by fabric width) strips.
  Subcut into 52 (2½" x 4½") G rectangles.
- Cut 10 (2½" by fabric width) strips.
  Subcut into 148 (2½") E squares.
- Cut 8 (2⅞" by fabric width) strips.
  Subcut into 100 (2⅞") squares. Cut each square on 1 diagonal to make 200 H triangles.
- Cut 4 (3⅜" by fabric width) strips.
  Subcut into 48 (3⅜") I squares.
- Cut 7 (2½" by fabric width) strips for N borders.

Completing the Half-Square Triangle Units

1. Select the A and B squares. Fold and press the A squares on both diagonals and in half vertically and horizontally to use lines as guides.

2. Open one A square, layering it over one B square with right sides together. Sew a ¼" seam on both sides of both diagonals as shown in Figure 1.

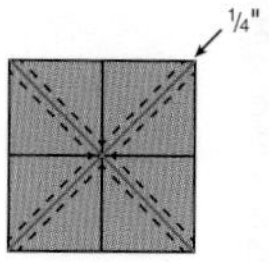

Figure 1

36

3. Cut stitched squares in half parallel to the edges in both directions, and then cut on both diagonals as shown in Figure 2. This will produce 8 A-B units.

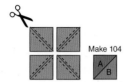

Make 104

Figure 2

4. Press each unit open with seam toward green. Trim all units to 3⅜" squares.

5. Repeat steps 1–4 with all A and B squares to make 104 A-B units.

Completing the Dark Gardenia Blocks

1. Join two A-B units to opposite sides of a C square as shown in Figure 3. Repeat to make 26 A-B-C units.

Make 26

Figure 3

2. Join two C squares to opposite sides of a D square as shown in Figure 4. Repeat to make 13 C-D units.

Make 13

Figure 4

3. Sew two A-B-C units to either sides of a C-D unit to complete a center unit as shown in Figure 5; press toward center row. Repeat to make 13 center units.

Make 13

Figure 5

4. Sew an F triangle to one side of an E square as shown in Figure 6. Press seam toward square.

Figure 6

5. Sew a G rectangle to the long side of the E-F unit as shown in Figure 7; press seam toward G.

Figure 7

6. Sew an H triangle to each end of E-F-G unit as shown in Figure 8. Press seam toward H to complete one corner unit.

Corner Unit
Make 52

Figure 8

7. Repeat steps 4–6 to make 52 corner units.

8. Sew a corner unit to opposite sides of the center unit as shown in Figure 9. Press seam toward center unit.

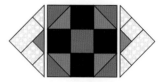

Figure 9

9. Complete the Dark Gardenia block by sewing a corner unit on the remaining two sides of the center unit referring to the block diagram. Repeat to make 13 blocks.

Completing the Light Gardenia Blocks

1. Join two A-B units to opposite sides of an I square as shown in Figure 10. Repeat to make 24 A-B-I units.

Make 24

Figure 10

2. Join two I squares to opposite sides of a D square as shown in Figure 11. Repeat to make 12 D-I units.

Make 12

Figure 11

3. Sew two A-B-I units to either sides of a D-I unit to complete a center unit as shown in Figure 12; press toward center row. Repeat to make 12 center units.

Make 12

Figure 12

4. Sew an E square to a J square as shown in Figure 13; press seam toward E. Add an H triangle to the E square, again referring to Figure 13. Repeat to make 48 E-H-J units.

Figure 13

5. Sew a K triangle to an E square as shown in Figure 14; press seam toward square. Repeat to make 48 E-K units.

Figure 14

6. Join an E-H-J unit with an E-K unit as shown in Figure 15. Press seam toward E-H-J unit.

Figure 15

7. Sew an H triangle to opposite end as shown in Figure 16 to complete one corner unit.

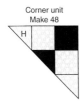

Figure 16

8. Repeat steps 6 and 7 to make 48 corner units.

9. Sew a corner unit to opposite sides of the center unit as shown in Figure 17. Press seam toward center unit.

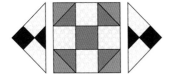

Figure 17

10. Complete the Light Gardenia block by sewing a corner unit on the remaining two sides of the center unit referring to the block diagram. Repeat to make 12 blocks.

Completing the Quilt

1. For Row 1, join three Dark Gardenia blocks with two Light Gardenia blocks, referring to Figure 18. Repeat to make three rows.

2. For Row 2 join two Dark Gardenia blocks with three Light Gardenia blocks, again referring to Figure 18. Repeat to make two rows.

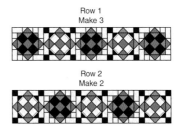

Figure 18

3. Join rows together, alternating Rows 1 and 2, referring to Assembly Diagram, to complete quilt center.

4. Join N border strips on short ends to make a long strip; press seams open. Subcut strip into four 60½" N strips. Sew two strips to the top and bottom of quilt center.

5. Sew an L square on both ends of the remaining N border strips. Sew to opposite sides of pieced center.

6. Join O border strips on short ends to make a long strip; press seams open. Subcut strips into four 64½" O strips. Sew two strips to the top and bottom of pieced center.

7. Sew an M square on both ends of the remaining O strips. Sew to opposite sides of pieced center.

8. Join P/Q strips on the short ends to make a long strip; press seams open. Subcut strip into two 68½" P strips and two 80½" Q strips.

9. Sew P strips to the top and bottom, and Q strips to opposite sides of pieced center.

10. Sandwich the batting between the pieced top and a prepared backing piece; baste layers together. Quilt as desired.

11. When quilting is complete, trim batting and backing fabric even with raw edges of the pieced top.

12. Prepare double-fold binding. Stitch binding to quilt front edges, mitering corners and overlapping ends. Fold binding to back side and stitch in place to finish. ■

"I spied a folding screen with a pattern that looked like a quilt block in the old film noir movie, The Blue Gardenia. I couldn't get that pattern out of my mind, so I started to fiddle around with it, and this design was born. So many designs can be born of this block, depending on where you place the values." —Lyn Brown

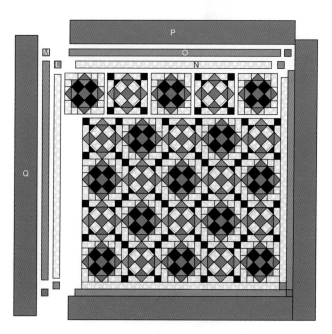

Blue Gardenia
Assembly Diagram 80" x 80"

Alternate Block Option

Blue Gardenia
Alternate Placement Diagram 56" x 80"
For this smaller size quilt, make 8 Dark Gardenia blocks and 7 Light Gardenia blocks. Arrange in 5 rows of 3 blocks each. Use the same borders as for the larger size.

Find the Stars Bed Runner

Designed & Quilted by Julia Dunn

Sometimes the options with a block are in the fabrics one chooses. This quilt only has one style of block, but imagine how different it could be in your fabrics. It's a basic paper-piecing project with lots of design possibilities.

Specifications
Skill Level: Intermediate
Quilt Size: 76" x 26"
Block Size: 10" x 10" finished
Number of Blocks: 14

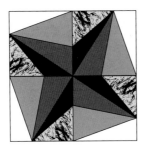

Star
10" x 10" Finished Block
Make 14

Materials
- ⅔ yard white
- 1 yard dark gray
- 1 yard medium gray
- 1 yard black print
- 2 yards black tonal
- Thread
- Backing to size
- Batting to size
- Basic sewing tools and supplies

Cutting

From black print:
- Cut 6 (1½" by fabric width) A/B border strips. Subcut two strips into two 22½" B strips.

From black tonal:
- Cut 6 (2½" by fabric width) C/D border strips. Subcut two strips into two 26½" D strips.
- Cut 6 (2¼" by fabric width) strips for binding.

Completing the Paper-Pieced Units
1. Make 56 same-size photocopies of the paper-piecing pattern given on page 42.

2. Complete 56 paper-pieced blocks referring to Paper Piecing tutorial on page 43.

Completing the Star Blocks
Note: Do not remove paper until after the borders are added to the pieced runner.

1. Join two paper-pieced units referring to Figure 1 for orientation for top row. Repeat for bottom row, again referring to Figure 1 for orientation.

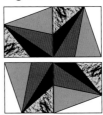

Figure 1

2. Join top and bottom rows to complete one Star block referring to block diagram.

3. Repeat steps 1 and 2 to make 14 Star blocks.

Completing the Runner
1. Arrange and join the Star blocks in two rows of seven blocks each referring to the Placement Diagram; press.

2. Join four A/B border strips together on short ends to make a long strip; press seams open. Subcut strip into two 70½" A strips.

3. Sew A strips to the top and bottom, and B strips to opposite sides of the pieced center.

4. Sew four C/D strips together on short ends to make a long strip; press seams open. Subcut strip into two 72½" C strips.

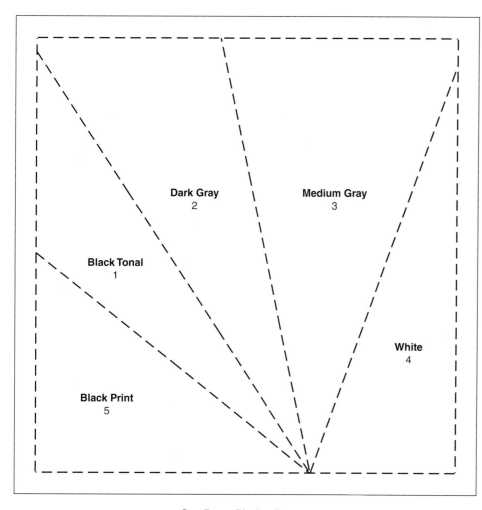

Star Paper-Piecing Pattern
Make 56 copies

5. Sew C strips to the top and bottom, and D strips to opposite sides of the pieced center.

6. Sandwich the batting between the pieced top and a prepared backing piece; baste layers together. Quilt as desired.

7. When quilting is complete, trim batting and backing fabric even with raw edges of the pieced top.

8. Prepare double-fold binding. Stitch binding to quilt front edges, mitering corners and overlapping ends. Fold binding to back side and stitch in place to finish. ■

"I have always loved stars and wanted to see if I could make one with other stars around that were made from the joining of the blocks. Have fun with your colors!" —Julia Dunn

Alternate Block Option

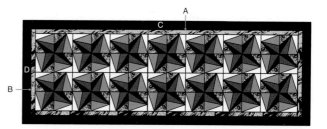

Find the Stars Bed Runner
Placement Diagram 76" x 26"

Find the Stars Table Runner
Alternate Placement Diagram 56" x 16"
To create this table runner, make 5 blocks and join them in 1 row. Add the same borders as on the original bed runner.

Paper Piecing

One of the oldest quilting techniques, paper piecing allows a quilter to make blocks with odd-shaped and/or small pieces. The paper is carefully removed when the block is completed. The following instructions are for one type of paper-piecing technique; refer to a comprehensive quilting guide for other types of paper piecing.

1. Make same-size photocopies of the paper-piecing pattern given as directed on the pattern. There are several choices in regular papers as well as water-soluble papers that can be used, which are available at your local office-supply store, quilt shop or online.

2. Cut out the patterns leaving a margin around the outside bold lines as shown in Figure 1. All patterns are reversed on the paper copies. Pattern color choices can be written in each numbered space on the marked side of each copy.

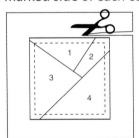

Figure 1

3. When cutting fabric for paper piecing, the pieces do not have to be the exact size and shape of the area to be covered. Cut fabric pieces the general shape and ¼"–½" larger than the design area to be covered. This makes paper-piecing a good way to use up scraps.

4. With the printed side of the pattern facing you, fold along each line of the pattern as shown in Figure 2, creasing the stitching lines. This will help in trimming the fabric seam allowances and in removing the paper when you are finished stitching.

Figure 2

5. Turn the paper pattern over with the unmarked side facing you and position fabric indicated on pattern right side up over the space marked 1. Hold the paper up to a window or over a light box to make sure that the fabric overlaps all sides of space 1 at least ¼" as shown in Figure 3 from the printed side of the pattern. Pin to hold fabric in place. ***Note:*** *You can also use a light touch of glue stick. Too much glue will make the paper difficult to remove.*

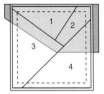

Figure 3

6. Turn the paper over with the right side of the paper facing you, and fold the paper along the lines between sections 1 and 2. Trim fabric to about ¼" from the folded edge as shown in Figure 4.

Figure 4

7. Place the second fabric indicated right sides together with first piece. Fabric edges should be even along line between spaces 1 and 2 as shown in Figure 5. Fold fabric over and check to see if second fabric piece will cover space 2.

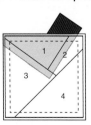

Figure 5

8. With the right side of the paper facing you, hold fabric pieces together and stitch along the line between spaces 1 and 2 as shown in Figure 6 using a very small stitch length (18–20 stitches per inch). ***Note:*** *Using a smaller stitch length will make removing paper easier because it creates a tear line at the seam.* Always begin and end seam by sewing two to three stitches beyond the line. You do not need to backstitch. When the beginning of the seam is at the edge of the pattern, start sewing at the solid outside line of the pattern.

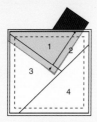

Figure 6

9. Turn the pattern over, flip the second fabric back and finger-press as shown in Figure 7.

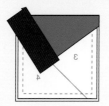

Figure 7

10. Continue trimming and sewing pieces in numerical order until the pattern is completely covered. Make sure pieces along the outer edge extend past the solid line to allow for a ¼" seam allowance as shown in Figure 8.

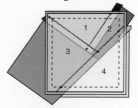

Figure 8

11. When the whole block is sewn, press the block and trim all excess fabric from the block along the outside-edge solid line of paper pattern as shown in Figure 9.

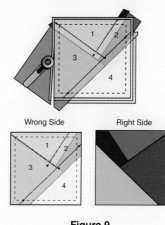

Wrong Side   Right Side

Figure 9

12. After stitching blocks together, carefully remove the backing paper from completed blocks and press seams. Or, staystitch ⅛" from the outer edge of the completed block. Carefully remove backing paper and press seams. Then complete quilt top assembly.

Row by Row

Design by Nancy Scott
Quilted by Masterpiece Quilting

Row quilts can be made either vertically or horizontally.
This is a great quilt pattern to experiment with color placement.

Specifications
Skill Level: Confident Beginner
Quilt Size: 72" x 72"
Block Size: 12" x 12" finished
Number of Blocks: 25

Materials
- 1⅝ yards white tonal*
- 2 yards gold tonal*
- 3⅔ yards gray tonal*
- Thread
- Backing to size
- Batting to size
- Basic sewing tools and supplies

Fabrics from Michael Miller.

Cutting

From white tonal:
- Cut 9 (3⅞" by fabric width) strips.
  Subcut into 90 (3⅞") C squares.
- Cut 1 (4¾" by fabric width) strip.
  Subcut into 5 (4¾") D squares.
- Cut 1 (6½" by fabric width) strip.
  Subcut into 5 (6½") E squares.

From gold tonal:
- Cut 15 (3⅞" by fabric width) strips.
  Subcut into 150 (3⅞") A squares.

From gray tonal:
- Cut 12 (3⅞" by fabric width) strips.
  Subcut into 120 (3⅞") B squares.
- Use remaining fabric length to cut the following strips.
  Cut 4 (6½" x 76") strips for F/G borders.
  Cut 4 (2¼" x 76") strips for binding.
  Cut 1 (3⅞" x 76") strip. Subcut into 10 (3⅞") B squares.

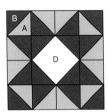

Mosaic 1
12" x 12" Finished Block
Make 5

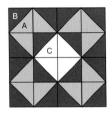

Mosaic 2
12" x 12" Finished Block
Make 5

Mosaic 3
12" x 12" Finished Block
Make 5

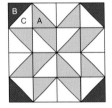

Mosaic 4
12" x 12" Finished Block
Make 5

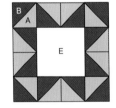

Mosaic 5
12" x 12" Finished Block
Make 5

Completing the Half-Square Triangle Units

1. Draw a diagonal line from corner to corner on the wrong side of 90 A squares.

2. Place an A square right sides together with a B square. Stitch ¼" on each side of the marked line as shown in Figure 1.

Figure 1

3. Cut the stitched unit apart on the marked line to make two A-B units as shown in Figure 2; press.

Make 180

Figure 2

4. Repeat steps 2 and 3 to make a total of 180 A-B units.

5. Draw a diagonal line from corner to corner on the wrong side of all C squares.

6. Place a C square right sides together with a B square. Stitch ¼" on each side of the marked line.

7. Cut the stitched unit apart on the marked line to make two B-C units as shown in Figure 3; press.

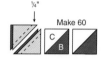

Figure 3

8. Repeat steps 6 and 7 to make a total of 60 B-C units.

9. Place a C square right sides together with an A square. Stitch ¼" on each side of the marked line.

10. Cut the stitched unit apart on the marked line to make two A-C units as shown in Figure 4; press.

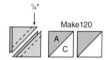

Figure 4

11. Repeat steps 9 and 10 to make a total of 120 A-C units.

Completing the Mosaic 1 Blocks

1. Select 12 A-B units, two B squares and one D square to complete one Mosaic 1 block.

2. Cut two B squares in half on 1 diagonal to make four B triangles. Sew two B triangles to opposite sides of D as shown in Figure 5; press seam toward B. Sew remaining two B triangles to remaining two sides of D to complete the B-D center unit; press seams toward B.

Figure 5

3. Join two A-B units along gold sides. Repeat to make four double A-B units as shown in Figure 6. Sew two of these units on either side of the B-D center unit to complete the center row as shown in Figure 7.

Figure 6

Figure 7

4. Sew A-B units to either end of the double A-B units to make the top row as shown in Figure 8. Repeat to make the bottom row.

Figure 8

5. Sew the top and bottom rows to the center row to complete one Mosaic 1 block referring to block diagram. Press all seams open.

6. Repeat steps 1–5 to complete a total of five Mosaic 1 blocks.

Completing the Mosaic 2 Blocks

1. Select 12 A-C units and four B-C units to complete one Mosaic 2 block.

2. Join two A-C units and two B-C units as shown in Figure 9 to make the top row. Repeat to make the bottom row.

Figure 9

3. Join four A-C units as shown in Figure 10 to make a center row. Repeat to make a second center row.

Figure 10

4. Join the two center rows referring to the block diagram. Sew the top and bottom rows to the center rows to complete the block.

5. Repeat steps 1–4 to complete a total of five Mosaic 2 blocks.

Completing the Mosaic 3 Blocks

1. Select 12 A-B units and four B-C units to complete one Mosaic 3 block.

2. Join the four B-C units, white sides together, as shown in Figure 11 for block center.

Figure 11

48

3. Join two A-B units along gray sides. Repeat to make four double A-B units as shown in Figure 12. Sew two of these units on either side of the block center to complete the center row as shown in Figure 13.

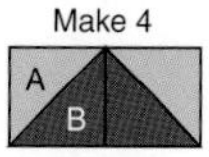

Make 4

Figure 12

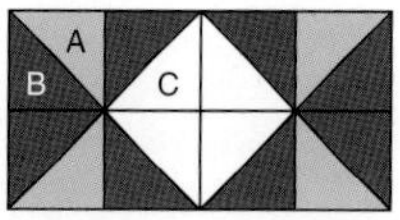

Figure 13

4. Sew two A-B units to either end of a double A-B unit as shown in Figure 14 to make a top row. Repeat to make a bottom row.

Figure 14

5. Sew the top and bottom rows to either side of the center row to complete the block, referring to the block diagram.

6. Repeat steps 1–5 to complete a total of five Mosaic 3 blocks.

Completing the Mosaic 4 Blocks

1. Select 12 A-C units and four B-C units to complete the Mosaic 4 block.

2. Join two A-C units and two B-C units as shown in Figure 15 to make the top row. Repeat to make the bottom row.

Figure 15

3. Join four A-C units as shown in Figure 16 to make a center row. Repeat to make a second center row.

Figure 16

4. Join the two center rows referring to the block diagram. Sew the top and bottom rows to center rows to complete block.

5. Repeat steps 1–4 to complete a total of five Mosaic 4 blocks.

Completing the Mosaic 5 Blocks

1. Select 12 A-B units and one E square to complete the Mosaic 5 block.

2. Join two A-B units along gold sides. Repeat to make four double A-B units as shown in Figure 17.

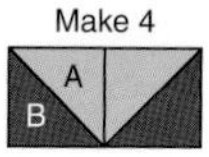

Make 4

Figure 17

3. Sew two double A-B units to opposite sides of the E square to form the center row as shown in Figure 18.

Figure 18

4. Sew A-B units to opposite ends of a double A-B unit to make a top row as shown in Figure 19. Repeat to make a bottom row.

Make 4

Figure 19

5. Sew the top and bottom rows to either side of the center row to complete the block, referring to the block diagram.

6. Repeat steps 1–5 to complete a total of five Mosaic 5 blocks.

Completing the Quilt

1. Join five identical blocks to form each row. Arrange and join the rows referring to Assembly Diagram. Press all seams open.

2. Trim the four border strips into two 60½" F strips and two 72½" G strips.

3. Sew F strips to the top and bottom of the pieced center and the G strips to opposite sides to complete the quilt top.

4. Sandwich the batting between the pieced top and a prepared backing piece; baste layers together. Quilt as desired.

5. When quilting is complete, trim batting and backing fabric even with raw edges of the pieced top.

6. Prepare double-fold binding. Stitch binding to quilt front edges, mitering corners and overlapping ends. Fold binding to back side and stitch in place to finish. ■

"I love designing simple quilts with lots of WOW! I was inspired by pairing traditional blocks with modern colors to create this quilt." —Nancy Scott

Row by Row
Assembly Diagram 72" x 72"

Alternate Block Options

Bow Tie Event

Designed & Quilted by Trice Boerens

Not every quilt block has to be square. Have fun with these easy rectangular blocks and the options you have in color and settings.

Specifications
Skill Level: Intermediate
Quilt Size: 63" x 67"
Block Size: 7" x 3" finished
Number of Blocks: 150

Materials
- ⅝ yard black solid
- ¾ yard red solid
- 1½ yards gray solid
- 1⅝ yards light peach solid
- 3⅓ yards yellow solid
- Thread
- Backing to size
- Batting to size
- Template material
- Basic sewing tools and supplies

Cutting

From black solid:
- Cut 5 (3½" by fabric width) strips.
  Subcut into 40 A pieces using pattern provided.

From red solid:
- Cut 5 (3½" by fabric width) strips.
  Subcut into 40 A pieces using pattern provided.
- Cut 4 C triangles using pattern provided.

From gray solid:
- Cut 18 (2¼" by fabric width) strips.
  Subcut into 260 B triangles using pattern provided.

From light peach solid:
- Cut 7 (4" by fabric width) strips for D/E borders.
- Cut 7 (2¼" by fabric width) strips for binding.

From yellow solid:
- Cut 27 (3½" by fabric width) strips.
  Subcut into 240 A pieces using pattern provided.
- Cut 6 (2¼" by fabric width) strips.
  Subcut into 80 B triangles using pattern provided.

Black Bow Tie
7" x 3" Finished Block
Make 20

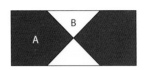

Red Bow Tie
7" x 3" Finished Block
Make 20

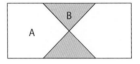

Yellow Bow Tie
7" x 3" Finished Block
Make 110

Completing the Bow Tie Blocks & End Units

1. Join one red A piece with a yellow B triangle as shown in Figure 1; press. Repeat to make a second A-B unit.

Figure 1

2. Join the two A-B units to complete one Red Bow Tie block referring to block diagram. Repeat to make a total of 20 Red Bow Tie blocks.

3. Repeat steps 1 and 2 using black A pieces and remaining yellow B triangles to make 20 Black Bow Tie blocks.

4. Repeat steps 1 and 2 using yellow A pieces and gray B triangles to make 110 Yellow Bow Tie blocks.

5. Join one yellow A piece with a gray B triangle; press. Sew a gray B triangle to the A-B unit as shown in Figure 2 to complete an end unit. Repeat to make a total of 20 end units.

Make 20

Figure 2

Completing the Quilt

1. Select and join two red blocks, two black blocks and four yellow blocks to make a horizontal row as shown in Figure 3. Repeat to make a total of 10 red/black/yellow rows, referring to the Assembly Diagram for the correct sequence of blocks for each row.

Figure 3

2. Join seven yellow blocks with two end units on both ends as shown in Figure 4. Repeat to make a total of 10 yellow rows.

Make 10

Figure 4

3. Join one red/black/yellow row to a yellow row as shown in Figure 5 centering the red/black/yellow row on the yellow row. Continue to join all rows referring to the Assembly Diagram for correct placement.

Figure 5

4. Trim end units on yellow rows even with the ends of red/black/yellow rows as shown in Figure 6 to complete quilt center.

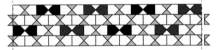

Figure 6

5. Join the D/E strips on the short ends to make a long strip; press. Subcut strip into two 63½" D strips and two 67½" E strips.

6. Center and sew the D strips to the top and bottom edge of the quilt top starting and stopping ¼" from each edge as shown in Figure 7. Center and sew the E strips to the sides of the quilt top in same manner, starting and stopping ¼" from each edge.

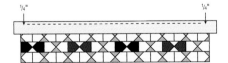

Figure 7

7. Miter each corner referring to Mitered Corner Borders on page 55.

8. Mark and trim each corner as shown in Figure 8. Sew a C triangle to each trimmed corner.

3½"

Figure 8

9. Sandwich the batting between the pieced top and a prepared backing piece; baste layers together. Quilt as desired.

10. When quilting is complete, trim batting and backing fabric even with raw edges of the pieced top.

11. Prepare double-fold binding. Stitch binding to quilt front edges, mitering corners and overlapping ends. Fold binding to back side and stitch in place to finish. ■

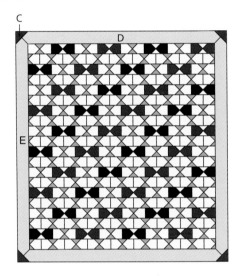

Bow Tie Event
Placement Diagram 63" x 67"

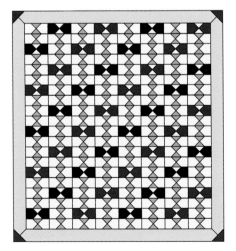

Bow Tie Event
Alternate Placement Diagram 63" x 67"
To create this new layout, you will not need any end units. Make 120 yellow bow tie blocks and make every other row 8 yellow blocks each. Add the same borders as on the original layout.

54

Alternate Block Options

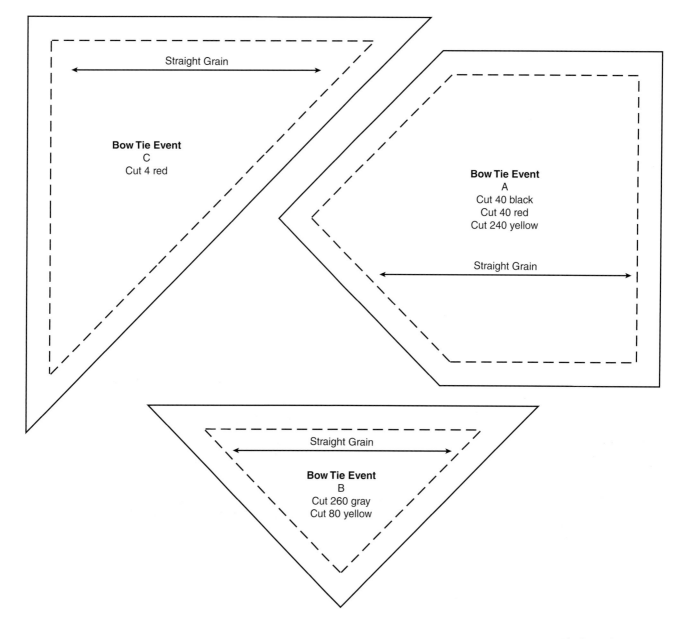

Bow Tie Event
C
Cut 4 red

Straight Grain

Bow Tie Event
A
Cut 40 black
Cut 40 red
Cut 240 yellow

Straight Grain

Bow Tie Event
B
Cut 260 gray
Cut 80 yellow

Straight Grain

Mitered Corner Borders

1. Add at least twice the border width to the border lengths measured or instructed to cut.

2. Center and sew the side borders to the quilt, beginning and ending stitching ¼" from the quilt corner and backstitching (Figure 1). Repeat with the top and bottom borders.

Figure 1

3. Fold and pin quilt right sides together at a 45-degree angle on one corner (Figure 2). Place a straightedge along the fold and lightly mark a line across the border ends.

Figure 2

4. Stitch along the line, backstitching to secure. Trim seam to ¼" and press open (Figure 3).

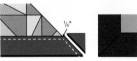

Figure 3

Special Thanks

Please join us in thanking the talented designers whose work is featured in this collection.

Photo Index

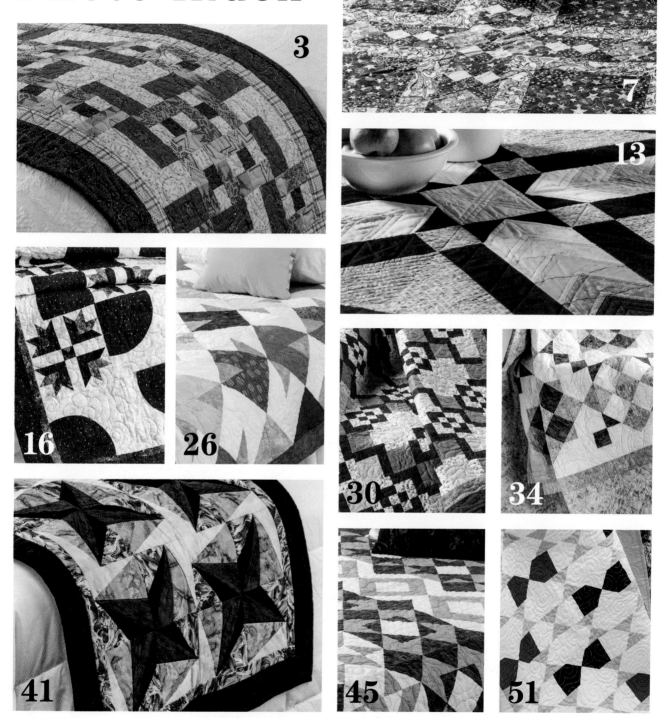

Blocks With Options is published by Annie's, 306 East Parr Road, Berne, IN 46711. Printed in USA. Copyright © 2013 Annie's. All rights reserved. This publication may not be reproduced in part or in whole without written permission from the publisher.

RETAIL STORES: If you would like to carry this pattern book or any other Annie's publication, visit AnniesWSL.com.

Every effort has been made to ensure that the instructions in this pattern book are complete and accurate. We cannot, however, take responsibility for human error, typographical mistakes or variations in individual work. Please visit AnniesCustomerCare.com to check for pattern updates.

ISBN: 978-1-59635-678-8

1 2 3 4 5 6 7 8 9